Welcome to your Journal.

The purpose of this journal is to help guide you through the coming year and help you to better understand the effects of the moon. Get comfortable and enjoy the journey!

This planner includes:
- Monthly Tracking of Moon Phases
- Journal Prompts for each Moon Phase
- Additional Daily Journal Pages

I hope this journal helps you to reach your highest potential this year through self-exploration, mindfulness and deep-thinking.

Please find our other books, journals and notebooks available on Amazon by searching for Mystic Tortoise.

Love and Light,
Mystic Tortoise

MOON PHASES

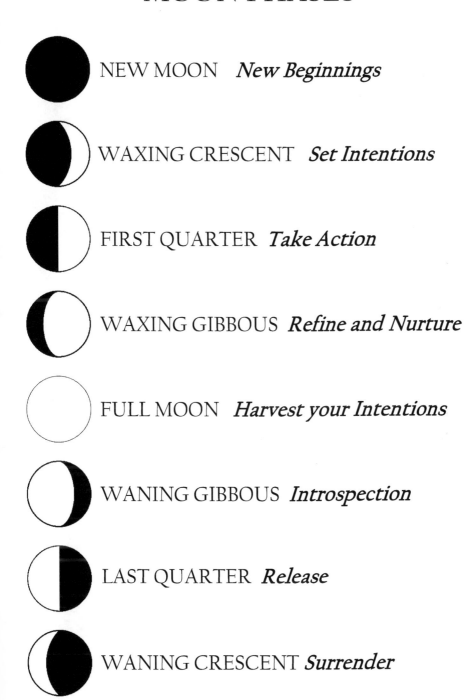

NEW MOON   *New Beginnings*

WAXING CRESCENT   *Set Intentions*

FIRST QUARTER   *Take Action*

WAXING GIBBOUS   *Refine and Nurture*

FULL MOON   *Harvest your Intentions*

WANING GIBBOUS   *Introspection*

LAST QUARTER   *Release*

WANING CRESCENT   *Surrender*

JANUARY 2020

1st-2nd	Waxing Crescent
3rd	First Quarter
4th-9th	Waxing Gibbous
10th	Full Moon
11th-16th	Waning Gibbous
17th	Last Quarter
18th-23rd	Waning Crescent
24th	New Moon
25th-31st	Waxing Crescent

FEBRUARY 2020

1st-2nd	First Quarter
3rd-8th	Waxing Gibbous
9th	Full Moon
10th-14th	Waning Gibbous
15th-16th	Last Quarter
17th-22nd	Waning Crescent
23rd	New Moon
24th-29th	Waxing Crescent

MARCH 2020

1st	Waxing Crescent
2nd	First Quarter
3rd-8th	Waxing Gibbous
9th	Full Moon
10th-15th	Waning Gibbous
16th	Last Quarter
17th-23rd	Waning Crescent
24th	New Moon
25th-31st	Waxing Crescent

APRIL 2020

1st	First Quarter
2nd-7th	Waxing Gibbous
8th	Full Moon
9th-13th	Waning Gibbous
14th-15th	Last Quarter
16th-22nd	Waning Crescent
23rd	New Moon
24th-29th	Waxing Crescent
30th	First Quarter

MAY 2020

1st-6th	Waxing Gibbous
7th	Full Moon
8th-13th	Waning Gibbous
14th	Last Quarter
15th-21st	Waning Crescent
22nd	New Moon
23rd-29th	Waxing Crescent
30th	First Quarter
31st	Waxing Gibbous

JUNE 2020

1st-4th	Waxing Gibbous
5th	Full Moon
6th-12th	Waning Gibbous
13th	Last Quarter
14th-20th	Waning Crescent
21st	New Moon
22nd-27th	Waxing Crescent
28th	First Quarter
29th-30th	Waxing Gibbous

JULY 2020

1st-4th	Waxing Gibbous
5th	Full Moon
6th-11th	Waning Gibbous
12th-13th	Last Quarter
14th-19th	Waning Crescent
20th	New Moon
21st-26th	Waxing Crescent
27th	First Quarter
28th-31st	Waxing Gibbous

AUGUST 2020

1st-2nd	Waxing Gibbous
3rd	Full Moon
4th-10th	Waning Gibbous
11th	Last Quarter
12th-18th	Waning Crescent
19th	New Moon
20th-24th	Waxing Crescent
25th	First Quarter
26th-31st	Waxing Gibbous

SEPTEMBER 2020

1st	Waxing Gibbous
2nd	Full Moon
3rd-9th	Waning Gibbous
10th	Last Quarter
11th-16th	Waning Crescent
17th	New Moon
18th-23rd	Waxing Crescent
24th	First Quarter
25th-30th	Waxing Gibbous

OCTOBER 2020

1st	Full Moon
2nd-8th	Waning Gibbous
9th-10th	Last Quarter
11th-15th	Waning Crescent
16th	New Moon
17th-22nd	Waxing Crescent
23rd	First Quarter
24th-30th	Waxing Gibbous
31st	Full Moon

NOVEMBER 2020

1st-7th	Waning Gibbous
8th	Last Quarter
9th-14th	Waning Crescent
15th	New Moon
16th-21st	Waxing Crescent
22nd	First Quarter
23rd-29th	Waxing Gibbous
30th	Full Moon

DECEMBER 2020

1st-6th	Waning Gibbous
7th-8th	Last Quarter
9th-13th	Waning Crescent
14th	New Moon
15th-20th	Waxing Crescent
21st-22nd	First Quarter
23rd-29th	Waxing Gibbous
30th	Full Moon
31st	Waning Gibbous

Journal: Strengths. Refine your visions.

 WAXING CRESCENT _____
                                      Date(s)

The Waxing Crescent Moon Phase represents setting intentions.

Intentions for this moon cycle

How am I feeling during this moon phase?

Where do I find inspiration? Why?

What is my body feeling right now?

Journal: Anxieties. Fears. Action plan to let them go.

_____

_____

_____

_____

_____

_____

_____

_____

_____

_____

_____

_____

_____

_____

_____

_____

_____

_____

_____

 FIRST QUARTER

_____
Date(s)

The First Quarter Moon represents a period of growth and action.

Action Items for this moon cycle

How am I feeling during this moon phase?

How have I been taking action towards my goals?

Are my actions aligned with the intentions I have set for myself?

Journal: Hopes and Outlook for the future

 WAXING GIBBOUS

_____
Date(s)

The Waxing Gibbous Moon represents a period of refining and nurturing your goals, hopes and dreams.

Intentions I want to nurture during this moon cycle

How am I feeling during this moon phase?

Which goals am I most excited about?

What is working for me? What is not? How can I improve?

Journal: Gratitude. All ways you have experienced abundance

 FULL MOON

_____
Date

The Full Moon represents a time to harvest your intentions that have been set and making sure they materialize.

What emotions am I feeling today?

What does my soul need?

What have I been neglecting?

What areas of my life feel out of alignment?

Journal: Wisdom and all the ways you are growing

 WANING GIBBOUS

Date(s) _____

The Waning Gibbous Moon represents a period of introspection and gratitude.

What am I grateful for?

How am I feeling during this moon phase?

How can I improve my mindfulness?

What new things have I learned about myself this cycle?

Journal: Negative energy you need to let go of

 LAST QUARTER

_____
Date(s)

The Last (Third) Quarter Moon represents a period of release and self-assessment.

What habits are stopping me from reaching my goals?

How am I feeling during this moon phase?

What could I have done differently during this cycle?

What am I holding on to that needs to be released?

Journal: Reflect on how far you have come this cycle

 WANING CRESCENT _____

Date(s)

The Waning Crescent Moon represents a period of surrender and a time for rest.

How can I improve my self-care?

How am I feeling during this moon phase?

What do I need to do for myself?

Is there anything in my life holding me back? How can I let go?

Journal: Hopes, Ambitions, and dreams

 NEW MOON

_____
Date

The New Moon represents a fresh start and new beginnings.

Goals for this moon cycle

How am I feeling during this moon phase?

How can I experience more joy and peace this month?

What in my life needs nourishment?

Journal: Anxieties. Fears. Action plan to let them go.

_____

_____

_____

_____

_____

_____

_____

_____

_____

_____

_____

_____

_____

_____

_____

_____

_____

_____

 FIRST QUARTER

_____
Date(s)

The First Quarter Moon represents a period of growth and action.

Action Items for this moon cycle

How am I feeling during this moon phase?

How have I been taking action towards my goals?

Are my actions aligned with the intentions I have set for myself?

Journal: Hopes and Outlook for the future

 WAXING GIBBOUS _____

Date(s)

The Waxing Gibbous Moon represents a period of refining and nurturing your goals, hopes and dreams.

Intentions I want to nurture during this moon cycle

How am I feeling during this moon phase?

Which goals am I most excited about?

What is working for me? What is not? How can I improve?

Journal: Gratitude. All ways you have experienced abundance

 FULL MOON

_____
Date

The Full Moon represents a time to harvest your intentions that have been set and making sure they materialize.

What emotions am I feeling today?

What does my soul need?

What have I been neglecting?

What areas of my life feel out of alignment?

Journal: Wisdom and all the ways you are growing

 WANING GIBBOUS

_____

Date(s)

The Waning Gibbous Moon represents a period of introspection and gratitude.

What am I grateful for?

How am I feeling during this moon phase?

How can I improve my mindfulness?

What new things have I learned about myself this cycle?

Journal: Negative energy you need to let go of

_____

_____

_____

_____

_____

_____

_____

_____

_____

_____

_____

_____

_____

_____

_____

_____

_____

_____

_____

_____

 LAST QUARTER

_____
Date(s)

The Last (Third) Quarter Moon represents a period of release and self-assessment.

What habits are stopping me from reaching my goals?

How am I feeling during this moon phase?

What could I have done differently during this cycle?

What am I holding on to that needs to be released?

Journal: Reflect on how far you have come this cycle

 WANING CRESCENT _____

Date(s)

The Waning Crescent Moon represents a period of surrender and a time for rest.

How can I improve my self-care?

How am I feeling during this moon phase?

What do I need to do for myself?

Is there anything in my life holding me back? How can I let go?

Journal: Hopes, Ambitions, and dreams

 NEW MOON

_____
Date

The New Moon represents a fresh start and new beginnings.

Goals for this moon cycle

How am I feeling during this moon phase?

How can I experience more joy and peace this month?

What in my life needs nourishment?

Journal: Strengths. Refine your visions.

 WAXING CRESCENT _____

Date(s)

The Waxing Crescent Moon Phase represents setting intentions.

Intentions for this moon cycle

How am I feeling during this moon phase?

Where do I find inspiration? Why?

What is my body feeling right now?

Journal: Anxieties. Fears. Action plan to let them go.

_____

_____

_____

_____

_____

_____

_____

_____

_____

_____

_____

_____

_____

_____

_____

_____

_____

_____

 FIRST QUARTER

_____
Date(s)

The First Quarter Moon represents a period of growth and action.

Action Items for this moon cycle

How am I feeling during this moon phase?

How have I been taking action towards my goals?

Are my actions aligned with the intentions I have set for myself?

Journal: Hopes and Outlook for the future

 WAXING GIBBOUS

Date(s) _____

The Waxing Gibbous Moon represents a period of refining and nurturing your goals, hopes and dreams.

Intentions I want to nurture during this moon cycle

How am I feeling during this moon phase?

Which goals am I most excited about?

What is working for me? What is not? How can I improve?

Journal: Gratitude. All ways you have experienced abundance

 FULL MOON

_____

Date

The Full Moon represents a time to harvest your intentions that have been set and making sure they materialize.

What emotions am I feeling today?

What does my soul need?

What have I been neglecting?

What areas of my life feel out of alignment?

Journal: Wisdom and all the ways you are growing

 WANING GIBBOUS _____

Date(s)

The Waning Gibbous Moon represents a period of introspection and gratitude.

What am I grateful for?

How am I feeling during this moon phase?

How can I improve my mindfulness?

What new things have I learned about myself this cycle?

Journal: Negative energy you need to let go of

 LAST QUARTER

_____
Date(s)

The Last (Third) Quarter Moon represents a period of release and self-assessment.

What habits are stopping me from reaching my goals?

How am I feeling during this moon phase?

What could I have done differently during this cycle?

What am I holding on to that needs to be released?

Journal: Reflect on how far you have come this cycle

 WANING CRESCENT _____

Date(s)

The Waning Crescent Moon represents a period of surrender and a time for rest.

How can I improve my self-care?

How am I feeling during this moon phase?

What do I need to do for myself?

Is there anything in my life holding me back? How can I let go?

Journal: Hopes, Ambitions, and dreams

 NEW MOON

_____
Date

The New Moon represents a fresh start and new beginnings.

Goals for this moon cycle

How am I feeling during this moon phase?

How can I experience more joy and peace this month?

What in my life needs nourishment?

Journal: Strengths. Refine your visions.

 WAXING CRESCENT _____

Date(s)

The Waxing Crescent Moon Phase represents setting intentions.

Intentions for this moon cycle

How am I feeling during this moon phase?

Where do I find inspiration? Why?

What is my body feeling right now?

Journal: Anxieties. Fears. Action plan to let them go.

 FIRST QUARTER

_____
Date(s)

The First Quarter Moon represents a period of growth and action.

Action Items for this moon cycle

How am I feeling during this moon phase?

How have I been taking action towards my goals?

Are my actions aligned with the intentions I have set for myself?

Journal: Hopes and Outlook for the future

 WAXING GIBBOUS

_____
Date(s)

The Waxing Gibbous Moon represents a period of refining and nurturing your goals, hopes and dreams.

Intentions I want to nurture during this moon cycle

How am I feeling during this moon phase?

Which goals am I most excited about?

What is working for me? What is not? How can I improve?

Journal: Gratitude. All ways you have experienced abundance

 FULL MOON

_____
Date

The Full Moon represents a time to harvest your intentions that have been set and making sure they materialize.

What emotions am I feeling today?

What does my soul need?

What have I been neglecting?

What areas of my life feel out of alignment?

Journal: Wisdom and all the ways you are growing

_____

_____

_____

_____

_____

_____

_____

_____

_____

_____

_____

_____

_____

_____

_____

_____

_____

_____

_____

_____

 WANING GIBBOUS _____

Date(s)

The Waning Gibbous Moon represents a period of introspection and gratitude.

What am I grateful for?

How am I feeling during this moon phase?

How can I improve my mindfulness?

What new things have I learned about myself this cycle?

Journal: Negative energy you need to let go of

 LAST QUARTER

_____

Date(s)

The Last (Third) Quarter Moon represents a period of release and self-assessment.

What habits are stopping me from reaching my goals?

How am I feeling during this moon phase?

What could I have done differently during this cycle?

What am I holding on to that needs to be released?

Journal: Reflect on how far you have come this cycle

 WANING CRESCENT

Date(s)

The Waning Crescent Moon represents a period of surrender and a time for rest.

How can I improve my self-care?

How am I feeling during this moon phase?

What do I need to do for myself?

Is there anything in my life holding me back? How can I let go?

Journal: Hopes, Ambitions, and dreams

 NEW MOON

_____
Date

The New Moon represents a fresh start and new beginnings.

Goals for this moon cycle

How am I feeling during this moon phase?

How can I experience more joy and peace this month?

What in my life needs nourishment?

Journal: Strengths. Refine your visions.

 WAXING CRESCENT _____
                                                    Date(s)

The Waxing Crescent Moon Phase represents setting intentions.

Intentions for this moon cycle

How am I feeling during this moon phase?

Where do I find inspiration? Why?

What is my body feeling right now?

Journal: Anxieties. Fears. Action plan to let them go.

_____

_____

_____

_____

_____

_____

_____

_____

_____

_____

_____

_____

_____

_____

_____

_____

_____

_____

_____

_____

_____

_____

 FIRST QUARTER

_____
Date(s)

The First Quarter Moon represents a period of growth and action.

Action Items for this moon cycle

How am I feeling during this moon phase?

How have I been taking action towards my goals?

Are my actions aligned with the intentions I have set for myself?

Journal: Hopes and Outlook for the future

 WAXING GIBBOUS _____

Date(s)

The Waxing Gibbous Moon represents a period of refining and nurturing your goals, hopes and dreams.

Intentions I want to nurture during this moon cycle

How am I feeling during this moon phase?

Which goals am I most excited about?

What is working for me? What is not? How can I improve?

Journal: Gratitude. All ways you have experienced abundance

 FULL MOON

_____
Date

The Full Moon represents a time to harvest your intentions that have been set and making sure they materialize.

What emotions am I feeling today?

What does my soul need?

What have I been neglecting?

What areas of my life feel out of alignment?

Journal: Wisdom and all the ways you are growing

 WANING GIBBOUS

_____
Date(s)

The Waning Gibbous Moon represents a period of introspection and gratitude.

What am I grateful for?

How am I feeling during this moon phase?

How can I improve my mindfulness?

What new things have I learned about myself this cycle?

Journal: Negative energy you need to let go of

 LAST QUARTER

Date(s) _____

The Last (Third) Quarter Moon represents a period of release and self-assessment.

What habits are stopping me from reaching my goals?

How am I feeling during this moon phase?

What could I have done differently during this cycle?

What am I holding on to that needs to be released?

Journal: Reflect on how far you have come this cycle

 WANING CRESCENT _____

Date(s)

The Waning Crescent Moon represents a period of surrender and a time for rest.

How can I improve my self-care?

How am I feeling during this moon phase?

What do I need to do for myself?

Is there anything in my life holding me back? How can I let go?

Journal: Hopes, Ambitions, and dreams

 NEW MOON

_____
Date

The New Moon represents a fresh start and new beginnings.

Goals for this moon cycle

How am I feeling during this moon phase?

How can I experience more joy and peace this month?

What in my life needs nourishment?

Journal: Strengths. Refine your visions.

 WAXING CRESCENT _____

Date(s)

The Waxing Crescent Moon Phase represents setting intentions.

Intentions for this moon cycle

How am I feeling during this moon phase?

Where do I find inspiration? Why?

What is my body feeling right now?

Journal: Anxieties. Fears. Action plan to let them go.

 FIRST QUARTER

_____
Date(s)

The First Quarter Moon represents a period of growth and action.

Action Items for this moon cycle

How am I feeling during this moon phase?

How have I been taking action towards my goals?

Are my actions aligned with the intentions I have set for myself?

Journal: Hopes and Outlook for the future

 WAXING GIBBOUS _____

Date(s)

The Waxing Gibbous Moon represents a period of refining and nurturing your goals, hopes and dreams.

Intentions I want to nurture during this moon cycle

How am I feeling during this moon phase?

Which goals am I most excited about?

What is working for me? What is not? How can I improve?

Journal: Gratitude. All ways you have experienced abundance

_____

_____

_____

_____

_____

_____

_____

_____

_____

_____

_____

_____

_____

_____

_____

_____

_____

_____

_____

_____

 FULL MOON

_____
Date

The Full Moon represents a time to harvest your intentions that have been set and making sure they materialize.

What emotions am I feeling today?

What does my soul need?

What have I been neglecting?

What areas of my life feel out of alignment?

Journal: Wisdom and all the ways you are growing

 WANING GIBBOUS _____

Date(s)

The Waning Gibbous Moon represents a period of introspection and gratitude.

What am I grateful for?

How am I feeling during this moon phase?

How can I improve my mindfulness?

What new things have I learned about myself this cycle?

Journal: Negative energy you need to let go of

 LAST QUARTER

_____
Date(s)

The Last (Third) Quarter Moon represents a period of release and self-assessment.

What habits are stopping me from reaching my goals?

How am I feeling during this moon phase?

What could I have done differently during this cycle?

What am I holding on to that needs to be released?

Journal: Reflect on how far you have come this cycle

WANING CRESCENT _____

Date(s)

The Waning Crescent Moon represents a period of surrender and a time for rest.

How can I improve my self-care?

How am I feeling during this moon phase?

What do I need to do for myself?

Is there anything in my life holding me back? How can I let go?

Journal: Hopes, Ambitions, and dreams

 NEW MOON

_____
Date

The New Moon represents a fresh start and new beginnings.

Goals for this moon cycle

How am I feeling during this moon phase?

How can I experience more joy and peace this month?

What in my life needs nourishment?

Journal: Strengths. Refine your visions.

_____

_____

_____

_____

_____

_____

_____

_____

_____

_____

_____

_____

_____

_____

_____

_____

_____

_____

_____

_____

 WAXING CRESCENT _____

Date(s)

The Waxing Crescent Moon Phase represents setting intentions.

Intentions for this moon cycle

How am I feeling during this moon phase?

Where do I find inspiration? Why?

What is my body feeling right now?

Journal: Anxieties. Fears. Action plan to let them go.

 FIRST QUARTER

_____
Date(s)

The First Quarter Moon represents a period of growth and action.

Action Items for this moon cycle

How am I feeling during this moon phase?

How have I been taking action towards my goals?

Are my actions aligned with the intentions I have set for myself?

Journal: Hopes and Outlook for the future

 WAXING GIBBOUS

_____
Date(s)

The Waxing Gibbous Moon represents a period of refining and nurturing your goals, hopes and dreams.

Intentions I want to nurture during this moon cycle

How am I feeling during this moon phase?

Which goals am I most excited about?

What is working for me? What is not? How can I improve?

Journal: Gratitude. All ways you have experienced abundance

_____

_____

_____

_____

_____

_____

_____

_____

_____

_____

_____

_____

_____

_____

_____

_____

_____

_____

_____

 FULL MOON

_____
Date

The Full Moon represents a time to harvest your intentions that have been set and making sure they materialize.

What emotions am I feeling today?

What does my soul need?

What have I been neglecting?

What areas of my life feel out of alignment?

Journal: Wisdom and all the ways you are growing

 WANING GIBBOUS _____

Date(s)

The Waning Gibbous Moon represents a period of introspection and gratitude.

What am I grateful for?

How am I feeling during this moon phase?

How can I improve my mindfulness?

What new things have I learned about myself this cycle?

Journal: Negative energy you need to let go of

 LAST QUARTER

_____
Date(s)

The Last (Third) Quarter Moon represents a period of release and self-assessment.

What habits are stopping me from reaching my goals?

How am I feeling during this moon phase?

What could I have done differently during this cycle?

What am I holding on to that needs to be released?

Journal: Reflect on how far you have come this cycle

 WANING CRESCENT _____
                                                    Date(s)

The Waning Crescent Moon represents a period of surrender and a time for rest.

How can I improve my self-care?

How am I feeling during this moon phase?

What do I need to do for myself?

Is there anything in my life holding me back? How can I let go?

Journal: Hopes, Ambitions, and dreams

 NEW MOON

_____
Date

The New Moon represents a fresh start and new beginnings.

Goals for this moon cycle

How am I feeling during this moon phase?

How can I experience more joy and peace this month?

What in my life needs nourishment?

Journal: Strengths. Refine your visions.

_____

_____

_____

_____

_____

_____

_____

_____

_____

_____

_____

_____

_____

_____

_____

_____

_____

_____

_____

_____

_____

 WAXING CRESCENT _____

Date(s)

The Waxing Crescent Moon Phase represents setting intentions.

Intentions for this moon cycle

How am I feeling during this moon phase?

Where do I find inspiration? Why?

What is my body feeling right now?

Journal: Anxieties. Fears. Action plan to let them go.

_____

_____

_____

_____

_____

_____

_____

_____

_____

_____

_____

_____

_____

_____

_____

_____

_____

_____

 FIRST QUARTER

_____
Date(s)

The First Quarter Moon represents a period of growth and action.

Action Items for this moon cycle

How am I feeling during this moon phase?

How have I been taking action towards my goals?

Are my actions aligned with the intentions I have set for myself?

Journal: Hopes and Outlook for the future

 WAXING GIBBOUS

Date(s) _____

The Waxing Gibbous Moon represents a period of refining and nurturing your goals, hopes and dreams.

Intentions I want to nurture during this moon cycle

How am I feeling during this moon phase?

Which goals am I most excited about?

What is working for me? What is not? How can I improve?

Journal: Gratitude. All ways you have experienced abundance

 FULL MOON

_____
Date

The Full Moon represents a time to harvest your intentions that have been set and making sure they materialize.

What emotions am I feeling today?

What does my soul need?

What have I been neglecting?

What areas of my life feel out of alignment?

Journal: Wisdom and all the ways you are growing

 WANING GIBBOUS   _____

Date(s)

The Waning Gibbous Moon represents a period of introspection and gratitude.

What am I grateful for?

How am I feeling during this moon phase?

How can I improve my mindfulness?

What new things have I learned about myself this cycle?

Journal: Negative energy you need to let go of

 LAST QUARTER

_____

Date(s)

The Last (Third) Quarter Moon represents a period of release and self-assessment.

What habits are stopping me from reaching my goals?

How am I feeling during this moon phase?

What could I have done differently during this cycle?

What am I holding on to that needs to be released?

Journal: Reflect on how far you have come this cycle

WANING CRESCENT _____

Date(s)

The Waning Crescent Moon represents a period of surrender and a time for rest.

How can I improve my self-care?

How am I feeling during this moon phase?

What do I need to do for myself?

Is there anything in my life holding me back? How can I let go?

Journal: Hopes, Ambitions, and dreams

 NEW MOON

_____
Date

The New Moon represents a fresh start and new beginnings.

Goals for this moon cycle

How am I feeling during this moon phase?

How can I experience more joy and peace this month?

What in my life needs nourishment?

Journal: Strengths. Refine your visions.

 WAXING CRESCENT _____

Date(s)

The Waxing Crescent Moon Phase represents setting intentions.

Intentions for this moon cycle

How am I feeling during this moon phase?

Where do I find inspiration? Why?

What is my body feeling right now?

Journal: Anxieties. Fears. Action plan to let them go.

 FIRST QUARTER

_____

Date(s)

The First Quarter Moon represents a period of growth and action.

Action Items for this moon cycle

How am I feeling during this moon phase?

How have I been taking action towards my goals?

Are my actions aligned with the intentions I have set for myself?

Journal: Hopes and Outlook for the future

 WAXING GIBBOUS   _____

Date(s)

The Waxing Gibbous Moon represents a period of refining and nurturing your goals, hopes and dreams.

Intentions I want to nurture during this moon cycle

How am I feeling during this moon phase?

Which goals am I most excited about?

What is working for me? What is not? How can I improve?

Journal: Gratitude. All ways you have experienced abundance

_____

_____

_____

_____

_____

_____

_____

_____

_____

_____

_____

_____

_____

_____

_____

_____

_____

_____

_____

_____

_____

_____

 FULL MOON

_____
Date

The Full Moon represents a time to harvest your intentions that have been set and making sure they materialize.

What emotions am I feeling today?

What does my soul need?

What have I been neglecting?

What areas of my life feel out of alignment?

Journal: Wisdom and all the ways you are growing

 WANING GIBBOUS

_____
Date(s)

The Waning Gibbous Moon represents a period of introspection and gratitude.

What am I grateful for?

How am I feeling during this moon phase?

How can I improve my mindfulness?

What new things have I learned about myself this cycle?

Journal: Negative energy you need to let go of

_____

_____

_____

_____

_____

_____

_____

_____

_____

_____

_____

_____

_____

_____

_____

_____

_____

_____

_____

_____

_____

_____

_____

 LAST QUARTER

_____
Date(s)

The Last (Third) Quarter Moon represents a period of release and self-assessment.

What habits are stopping me from reaching my goals?

How am I feeling during this moon phase?

What could I have done differently during this cycle?

What am I holding on to that needs to be released?

Journal: Reflect on how far you have come this cycle

 WANING CRESCENT _____

Date(s)

The Waning Crescent Moon represents a period of surrender and a time for rest.

How can I improve my self-care?

How am I feeling during this moon phase?

What do I need to do for myself?

Is there anything in my life holding me back? How can I let go?

Journal: Hopes, Ambitions, and dreams

NEW MOON

_____
Date

The New Moon represents a fresh start and new beginnings.

Goals for this moon cycle

How am I feeling during this moon phase?

How can I experience more joy and peace this month?

What in my life needs nourishment?

Journal: Strengths. Refine your visions.

 WAXING CRESCENT _____
                                        Date(s)

The Waxing Crescent Moon Phase represents setting intentions.

Intentions for this moon cycle

How am I feeling during this moon phase?

Where do I find inspiration? Why?

What is my body feeling right now?

Journal: Anxieties. Fears. Action plan to let them go.

 FIRST QUARTER

_____
Date(s)

The First Quarter Moon represents a period of growth and action.

Action Items for this moon cycle

How am I feeling during this moon phase?

How have I been taking action towards my goals?

Are my actions aligned with the intentions I have set for myself?

Journal: Hopes and Outlook for the future

 WAXING GIBBOUS

_____

Date(s)

The Waxing Gibbous Moon represents a period of refining and nurturing your goals, hopes and dreams.

Intentions I want to nurture during this moon cycle

How am I feeling during this moon phase?

Which goals am I most excited about?

What is working for me? What is not? How can I improve?

Journal: Gratitude. All ways you have experienced abundance

_____

_____

_____

_____

_____

_____

_____

_____

_____

_____

_____

_____

_____

_____

_____

_____

_____

_____

 FULL MOON

_____
Date

The Full Moon represents a time to harvest your intentions that have been set and making sure they materialize.

What emotions am I feeling today?

What does my soul need?

What have I been neglecting?

What areas of my life feel out of alignment?

Journal: Wisdom and all the ways you are growing

 WANING GIBBOUS _____

Date(s)

The Waning Gibbous Moon represents a period of introspection and gratitude.

What am I grateful for?

How am I feeling during this moon phase?

How can I improve my mindfulness?

What new things have I learned about myself this cycle?

Journal: Negative energy you need to let go of

 LAST QUARTER

_____

Date(s)

The Last (Third) Quarter Moon represents a period of release and self-assessment.

What habits are stopping me from reaching my goals?

How am I feeling during this moon phase?

What could I have done differently during this cycle?

What am I holding on to that needs to be released?

Journal: Reflect on how far you have come this cycle

_____

_____

_____

_____

_____

_____

_____

_____

_____

_____

_____

_____

_____

_____

_____

_____

_____

_____

 WANING CRESCENT _____

Date(s)

The Waning Crescent Moon represents a period of surrender and a time for rest.

How can I improve my self-care?

How am I feeling during this moon phase?

What do I need to do for myself?

Is there anything in my life holding me back? How can I let go?

Journal: Hopes, Ambitions, and dreams

 NEW MOON

_____
Date

The New Moon represents a fresh start and new beginnings.

Goals for this moon cycle

How am I feeling during this moon phase?

How can I experience more joy and peace this month?

What in my life needs nourishment?

Journal: Strengths. Refine your visions.

 WAXING CRESCENT _____

Date(s)

The Waxing Crescent Moon Phase represents setting intentions.

Intentions for this moon cycle

How am I feeling during this moon phase?

Where do I find inspiration? Why?

What is my body feeling right now?

Journal: Anxieties. Fears. Action plan to let them go.

 FIRST QUARTER

_____

Date(s)

The First Quarter Moon represents a period of growth and action.

Action Items for this moon cycle

How am I feeling during this moon phase?

How have I been taking action towards my goals?

Are my actions aligned with the intentions I have set for myself?

Journal: Hopes and Outlook for the future

 WAXING GIBBOUS _____

Date(s)

The Waxing Gibbous Moon represents a period of refining and nurturing your goals, hopes and dreams.

Intentions I want to nurture during this moon cycle

How am I feeling during this moon phase?

Which goals am I most excited about?

What is working for me? What is not? How can I improve?

Journal: Gratitude. All ways you have experienced abundance

 FULL MOON

_____
Date

The Full Moon represents a time to harvest your intentions that have been set and making sure they materialize.

What emotions am I feeling today?

What does my soul need?

What have I been neglecting?

What areas of my life feel out of alignment?

Journal: Wisdom and all the ways you are growing

 WANING GIBBOUS _____

Date(s)

The Waning Gibbous Moon represents a period of introspection and gratitude.

What am I grateful for?

How am I feeling during this moon phase?

How can I improve my mindfulness?

What new things have I learned about myself this cycle?

Journal: Negative energy you need to let go of

 LAST QUARTER

_____
Date(s)

The Last (Third) Quarter Moon represents a period of release and self-assessment.

What habits are stopping me from reaching my goals?

How am I feeling during this moon phase?

What could I have done differently during this cycle?

What am I holding on to that needs to be released?

Journal: Reflect on how far you have come this cycle

 WANING CRESCENT _____

Date(s)

The Waning Crescent Moon represents a period of surrender and a time for rest.

How can I improve my self-care?

How am I feeling during this moon phase?

What do I need to do for myself?

Is there anything in my life holding me back? How can I let go?

Journal: Hopes, Ambitions, and dreams

 NEW MOON

_____
Date

The New Moon represents a fresh start and new beginnings.

Goals for this moon cycle

How am I feeling during this moon phase?

How can I experience more joy and peace this month?

What in my life needs nourishment?

Journal: Strengths. Refine your visions.

# WAXING CRESCENT

Date(s)

The Waxing Crescent Moon Phase represents setting intentions.

Intentions for this moon cycle

How am I feeling during this moon phase?

Where do I find inspiration? Why?

What is my body feeling right now?

Journal: Anxieties. Fears. Action plan to let them go.

 FIRST QUARTER

_____
Date(s)

The First Quarter Moon represents a period of growth and action.

Action Items for this moon cycle

How am I feeling during this moon phase?

How have I been taking action towards my goals?

Are my actions aligned with the intentions I have set for myself?

Journal: Hopes and Outlook for the future

 WAXING GIBBOUS _____

Date(s)

The Waxing Gibbous Moon represents a period of refining and nurturing your goals, hopes and dreams.

Intentions I want to nurture during this moon cycle

How am I feeling during this moon phase?

Which goals am I most excited about?

What is working for me? What is not? How can I improve?

Journal: Gratitude. All ways you have experienced abundance

 FULL MOON

_____
Date

The Full Moon represents a time to harvest your intentions that have been set and making sure they materialize.

What emotions am I feeling today?

What does my soul need?

What have I been neglecting?

What areas of my life feel out of alignment?

Journal: Wisdom and all the ways you are growing

 WANING GIBBOUS

Date(s) _____

The Waning Gibbous Moon represents a period of introspection and gratitude.

What am I grateful for?

How am I feeling during this moon phase?

How can I improve my mindfulness?

What new things have I learned about myself this cycle?

Journal: Negative energy you need to let go of

 LAST QUARTER

_____

Date(s)

The Last (Third) Quarter Moon represents a period of release and self-assessment.

What habits are stopping me from reaching my goals?

How am I feeling during this moon phase?

What could I have done differently during this cycle?

What am I holding on to that needs to be released?

Journal: Reflect on how far you have come this cycle

 WANING CRESCENT _____

Date(s)

The Waning Crescent Moon represents a period of surrender and a time for rest.

How can I improve my self-care?

How am I feeling during this moon phase?

What do I need to do for myself?

Is there anything in my life holding me back? How can I let go?

Journal: Hopes, Ambitions, and dreams

 NEW MOON

_____

Date

The New Moon represents a fresh start and new beginnings.

Goals for this moon cycle

How am I feeling during this moon phase?

How can I experience more joy and peace this month?

What in my life needs nourishment?

Journal: Strengths. Refine your visions.

WAXING CRESCENT _____

Date(s)

The Waxing Crescent Moon Phase represents setting intentions.

Intentions for this moon cycle

How am I feeling during this moon phase?

Where do I find inspiration? Why?

What is my body feeling right now?

Journal: Anxieties. Fears. Action plan to let them go.

_____

_____

_____

_____

_____

_____

_____

_____

_____

_____

_____

_____

_____

_____

_____

_____

_____

_____

_____

 FIRST QUARTER

_____

Date(s)

The First Quarter Moon represents a period of growth and action.

Action Items for this moon cycle

How am I feeling during this moon phase?

How have I been taking action towards my goals?

Are my actions aligned with the intentions I have set for myself?

Journal: Hopes and Outlook for the future

 WAXING GIBBOUS _____

Date(s)

The Waxing Gibbous Moon represents a period of refining and nurturing your goals, hopes and dreams.

Intentions I want to nurture during this moon cycle

How am I feeling during this moon phase?

Which goals am I most excited about?

What is working for me? What is not? How can I improve?

Journal: Gratitude. All ways you have experienced abundance

 FULL MOON

_____
Date

The Full Moon represents a time to harvest your intentions that have been set and making sure they materialize.

What emotions am I feeling today?

What does my soul need?

What have I been neglecting?

What areas of my life feel out of alignment?

Journal: Wisdom and all the ways you are growing

 WANING GIBBOUS

_____
Date(s)

The Waning Gibbous Moon represents a period of introspection and gratitude.

What am I grateful for?

How am I feeling during this moon phase?

How can I improve my mindfulness?

What new things have I learned about myself this cycle?

Made in the USA
San Bernardino, CA
15 January 2020